j602
S21d

DETROIT PUBLIC LIBRARY

☞ **W9-BXF-670**

026083791

DETROIT PUBLIC LIBRARY

CHILDREN'S LIBRARY

DATE DUE

	FEB 1 9 2000
SEP 2 6 1997	
APR 2 3 1998	
JUN 0 3 1998	
AUG 0 6 1998	
NOV 26 1999	

BC-3

CL

DRAW, MODEL, & PAINT

DRAGONS and PREHISTORIC MONSTERS

by Isidro Sánchez
Models by Roser Piñol
Photographs by Juan Carlos Martínez

Gareth Stevens Publishing
MILWAUKEE

For a free color catalog describing Gareth Stevens' list of high-quality books,
call 1-800-542-2595 (USA) or 1-800-461-9120 (Canada).
Gareth Stevens' Fax: 414-225-0377.

Library of Congress Cataloging-in-Publication Data

Sánchez, Isidro.
    [Dragones y monstruos prehistóricos. English]
    Dragons and prehistoric monsters / text by Isidro Sánchez ; models by Roser Piñol ;
photography by Juan Carlos Martínez.
      p. cm. — (Draw, model, and paint)
    Includes index.
    Summary: Presents instructions for making dragons, a woolly mammoth, prehistoric fish,
and other creatures from materials such as modeling clay, Plaster of Paris, and posterboard.
    ISBN 0-8368-1521-1 (lib. bdg.)
    1. Dragons in art—Juvenile literature. 2. Monsters of art—Juvenile literature.
3. Sculpture—Juvenile literature. [1. Dragons in art. 2. Monsters in art. 3. Sculpture.]
I. Piñol, Roser. II. Martínez, Juan Carlos, 1944- ill. III. Title. IV. Series.
NB1143.S26   1996
745.592—dc20   95-43908

This North American edition first published in 1996 by
Gareth Stevens Publishing
1555 North RiverCenter Drive, Suite 201
Milwaukee, Wisconsin 53212, USA

Original edition © 1995 Ediciones Este, S.A., Barcelona, Spain, under the title
Dragones Y Monstruos Prehistóricos. Text by Isidro Sánchez. Models by Roser
Piñol. Photography by Juan Carlos Martínez. All additional material supplied
for this edition © 1996 by Gareth Stevens, Inc.

All rights to this edition reserved to Gareth Stevens, Inc. No part of this book may
be reproduced, stored in a retrieval system, or transmitted in any form or by any
means, electronic, mechanical, photocopying, recording, or otherwise without the
prior written permission of the publisher except for the inclusion of brief quotations
in an acknowledged review.

Series editor: Barbara J. Behm
Editorial assistants: Jamie Daniel, Diane Laska, Rita Reitci

Printed in the United States of America

1 2 3 4 5 6 7 8 9 99 98 97 96

CONTENTS

A two-headed dragon

Celebrations in China feature spectacular fireworks and colorful dragons. The dragons, such as this two-headed creature, have been inspired by Chinese legends.

You will need:
- thin wooden sticks
- palette knives
- modeling clay
- colored pins

1. Shape a piece of green modeling clay like this for the main part of the dragon's body.

2. Shape two smaller pieces and flatten them with the palm of your hand to make the dragon's wings.

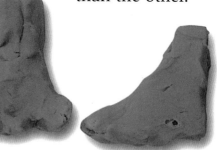

4. Roll out four short pieces. Shape them to look like legs, shown below.

3. Roll out a long piece for the tail. Make one end wider than the other.

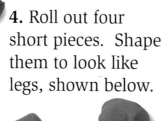

5. Roll out two longer rolls of clay for the two necks.

6. Insert a stick in the bottom of each neck.

7. Insert a stick in the tail.

8. Attach the tail to the main part of the body.

9. Shape the feet. Make the toes by cutting away clay with a palette knife.

10. Flatten the wings a little more, and shape them with your fingers.

11. Join the rest of the parts to the main body. To attach the pieces that do not have sticks, gently pinch the clay together.

12. Smooth the dragon's entire body with the palette knife. Also use the knife to add texture to the dragon's skin. To do this, gently push the point of the knife into the clay to make a pattern, as shown.

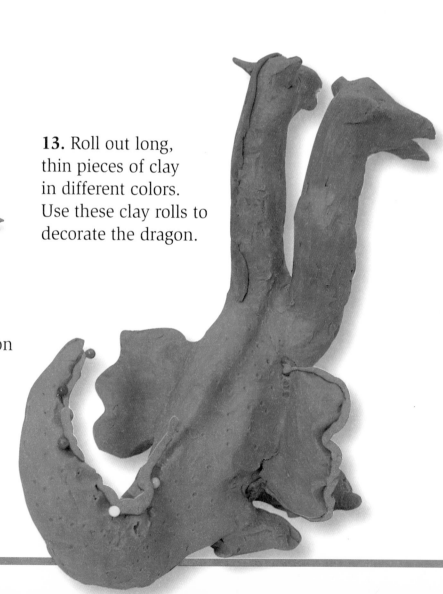

13. Roll out long, thin pieces of clay in different colors. Use these clay rolls to decorate the dragon.

14. Decorate the front of the dragon with little balls of clay in various colors and sizes. Gently press them into the dragon.

15. Add black and white balls of clay for the eyes. Add a red nose and small pieces of white clay for the teeth and claws. Finish the dragon by decorating the heads and tail with colored pins.

A woolly mammoth

The woolly mammoth was a prehistoric mammal that looked like one of today's elephants. About ten thousand years ago, the woolly mammoth became extinct. It was about 15 feet (4.5 meters) tall and had powerful tusks almost 13 feet (4 m) long. It lived in Europe, Asia, and North America at the same time as prehistoric people. These people hunted the woolly mammoth for food and painted pictures of the animal on the walls of their cave dwellings.

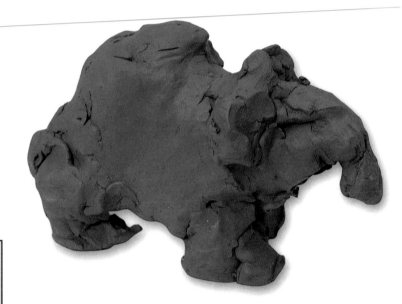

You will need:
- "slip," which is made by mixing small chunks of clay with water until a paste forms
- a paintbrush
- modeling clay (brown)
- palette knives
- tempera paints

1. Shape a piece of brown clay to look like a mammoth's body, head, and feet.

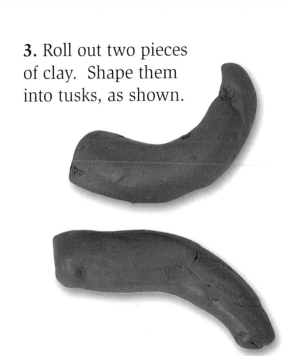

3. Roll out two pieces of clay. Shape them into tusks, as shown.

2. The legs need to be wide and sturdy to support such a large animal. Use a palette knife to scrape away clay in order to get the desired shape of the legs.

4. Carefully attach the tusks to the mammoth with a little slip. Then smooth the area with a palette knife.

6. Paint the mammoth dark brown except for its eyes and tusks.

5. Add texture to the mammoth by carefully making small slices in the body with the end of a palette knife. This will give the appearance of thick, coarse hair. Then, let the clay dry.

7. After the paint dries, paint some orange and green patches on the animal's back and the rear of the legs.

8. The other side of the mammoth is shown above.

9. Paint the tusks yellow or light brown. Make light brown paint by mixing some white into brown. Add any final touches with other colors of paint.

A prehistoric fish

Among the first inhabitants of the prehistoric oceans were ferocious armored fish. They lived over 350 million years ago. Their bodies were covered with hard, thick plates of bone. Some were nearly 30 feet (9 m) long!

You will need:
- cardboard
- red posterboard
- a drinking straw
- papier-mâché (from an art supply store)
- old newspapers or magazines
- glue
- scissors
- tape
- a pencil
- a paintbrush
- a black felt-tip pen
- tempera paints

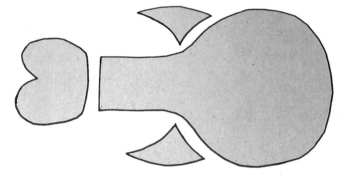

1. With a pencil, draw the main outline of the fish on cardboard. Then, go over the drawing with a black felt-tip pen.

2. Cut out the pieces with scissors.

4. This is how the fish should look once it has been completely covered and taped.

3. With tape, attach the fins and tail to the main body. Crumple newspaper or magazine paper into tight balls. Tape them to the body, as shown.

5. Follow the directions on the package for mixing papier-mâché. Spread papier-mâché over the fish with your fingers. Don't put it on too thickly; use just enough to cover the paper.

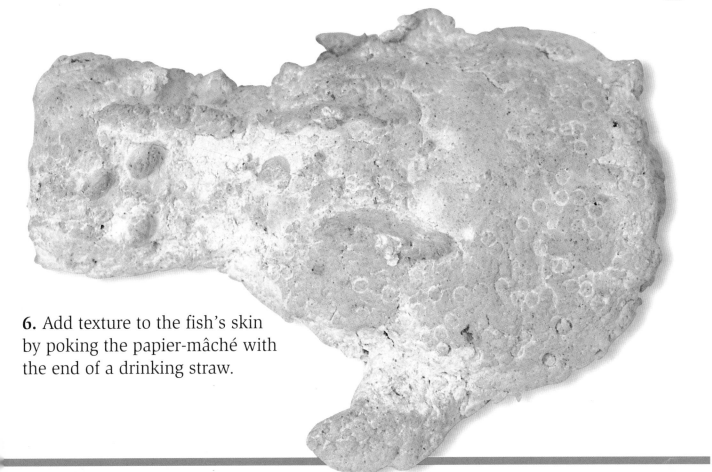

6. Add texture to the fish's skin by poking the papier-mâché with the end of a drinking straw.

10. Outline the blue patches with white.

9. When the blue paint is dry, paint the eyes white. Add lines of white to the tail and fins.

8. Paint the fins blue. Add blue patches and spots to the main body. Paint a blue line down the center of the tail.

7. Mix white and black paint to make gray. Paint the fish gray except for the inside of the mouth. Let the paint dry. Always wash your paintbrush between colors.

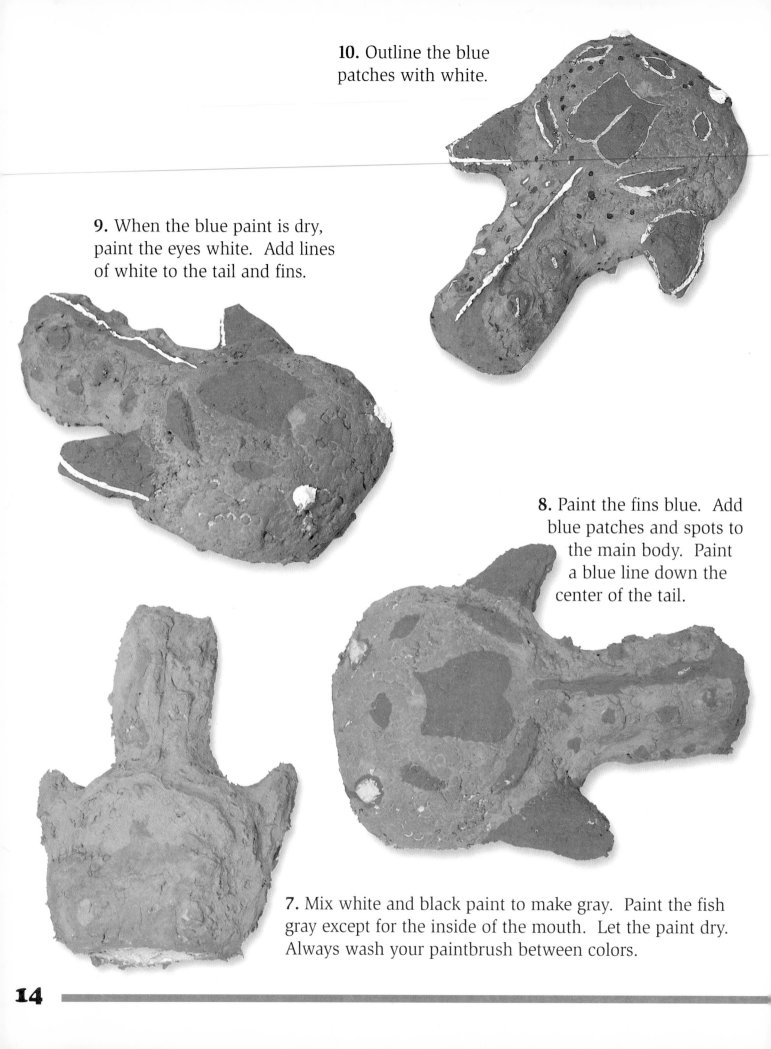

11. Add light blue spots next to the dark blue spots.

12. Paint the inside of the mouth red. When the paint is dry, cut out a tongue shape from the red posterboard. Glue it into place.

A Spanish dragon

A certain Spanish dragon is famous throughout the world. It was created by the Spanish architect Antoni Gaudi, who lived from 1852-1926. Gaudi's dragon is made of many differently colored pieces of ceramic tile. The tiles, which come in various shapes and sizes, have been placed together carefully like a big jigsaw puzzle.

1. From a block of brown clay, shape the figure shown below. Use a palette knife to carefully remove any unwanted clay from around the legs and tail.

2. Continue to shape the dragon with your hands.

3. Make wavy lines in the clay by pressing into the clay with the tips of your fingers. Shape the mouth by removing clay from the head with a palette knife. Next, shape the dragon's claws with a palette knife.

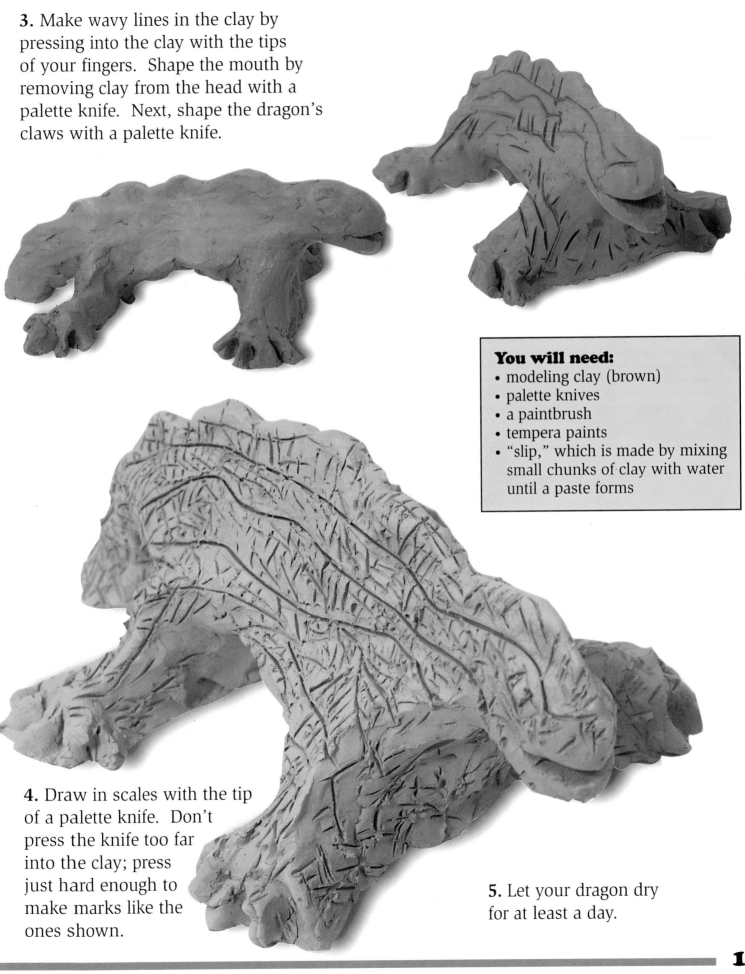

You will need:
- modeling clay (brown)
- palette knives
- a paintbrush
- tempera paints
- "slip," which is made by mixing small chunks of clay with water until a paste forms

4. Draw in scales with the tip of a palette knife. Don't press the knife too far into the clay; press just hard enough to make marks like the ones shown.

5. Let your dragon dry for at least a day.

A medieval dragon

In the Middle Ages, people believed in dragons with long tails, enormous clawed feet, and wings. They even imagined dragons that breathed fire!

You will need:
- cardboard
- Plaster of Paris roll
- a black felt-tip pen
- Popsicle sticks
- newspaper or magazine paper
- scissors
- tape
- a pencil
- red tissue paper
- a paintbrush
- tempera paints

1. On a piece of cardboard, draw the main body, wings, crests, and feet of the dragon with a pencil. Go over the outline with a black felt-tip pen.

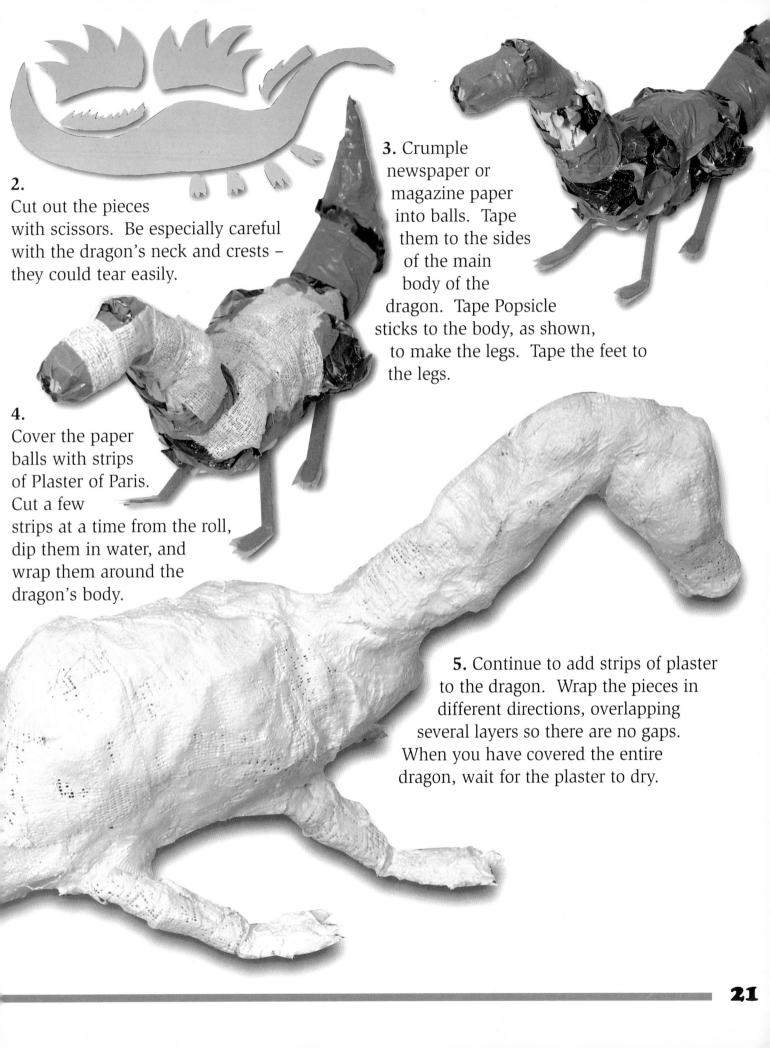

2.
Cut out the pieces with scissors. Be especially careful with the dragon's neck and crests – they could tear easily.

3. Crumple newspaper or magazine paper into balls. Tape them to the sides of the main body of the dragon. Tape Popsicle sticks to the body, as shown, to make the legs. Tape the feet to the legs.

4.
Cover the paper balls with strips of Plaster of Paris. Cut a few strips at a time from the roll, dip them in water, and wrap them around the dragon's body.

5. Continue to add strips of plaster to the dragon. Wrap the pieces in different directions, overlapping several layers so there are no gaps. When you have covered the entire dragon, wait for the plaster to dry.

8. Tape the crests to the body, and cover them with plaster. When the plaster dries, you are ready to paint. Paint a thick coat of dark green on the areas of the dragon shown at right.

7. Cover the wings with thin plaster strips that you have dipped in water. Overlap the strips in different directions.

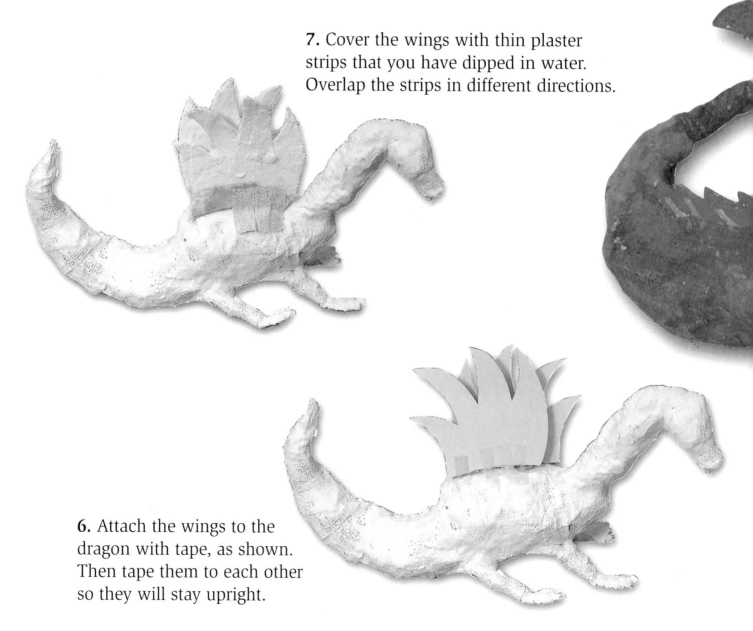

6. Attach the wings to the dragon with tape, as shown. Then tape them to each other so they will stay upright.

9. Paint most of the tail and head dark green, as shown. Mix a little white into the dark green paint to make light green. Use light green on the crest of the neck and the edges of the wings. Be sure the first color of paint has dried before adding the next color, so they don't run together.

Always wash your brush between colors.

10. Paint the tips of the wings and the crest of the tail blue. Add various other colors if you like. Use red for the tongue and black and white for the eyes.

11. Dangle some red tissue paper from the dragon's mouth, and it will breathe fire!

A Chinese dragon

In many Asian countries, such as China and Japan, it has been traditional for centuries to create and decorate dragons. Bamboo, tissue paper, and rice paper dragons are painted in bright colors.

The annual boat races on the Yellow River in China feature boats decorated as huge dragons. The dragon you are about to make brings together three elements that have always been part of Chinese dragon decorating – brilliant color, beautiful design, and lots of imagination.

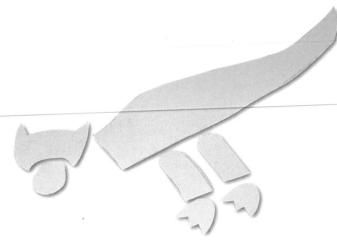

1. Draw the main body, tail, head, legs, and feet of the dragon onto cardboard with a pencil. Go over the outline with a black felt-tip pen. Then, cut the pieces out with scissors.

You will need:
- cardboard
- art paste
- a black felt-tip pen
- colored stones, beads, etc.
- newspaper or magazine paper
- tape
- scissors
- a paintbrush
- a pencil
- tempera paints
- shells
- feathers

2. Tape the pieces of the dragon together. Crumple newspaper or magazine paper into balls. Make as many balls as you need to give the dragon's body a solid shape.

3. Attach the balls to the cardboard with tape, as shown.

4. Cover the dragon's midsection, tail, head, and feet entirely. Remember to do both sides.

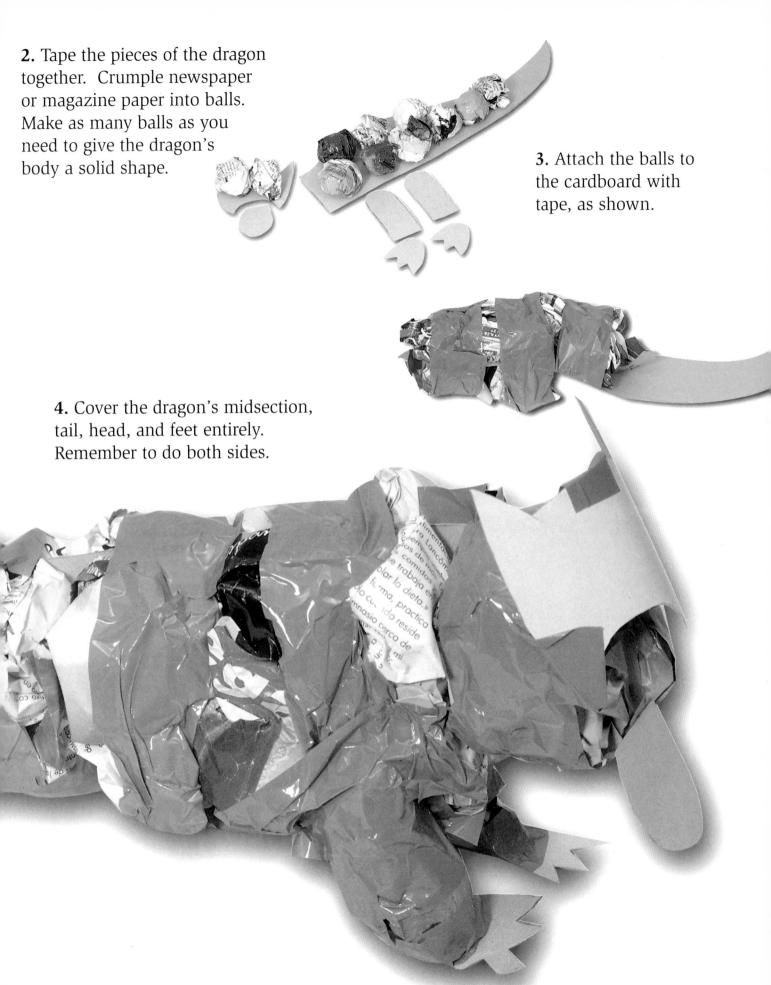

5. Dissolve a little art paste in water until there are no lumps. Cover the dragon with the paste. Dip strips of newspaper in the paste for just a moment. Then place the strips on the frame of the dragon.

6. Continue placing the strips in different directions until the entire frame is covered. Then let it dry.

7. Now you can start painting. Remember to wash your paintbrush after each color.

8. Paint one color and one section of the dragon at a time. This way, the colors won't run together. When the dragon is painted and dry, you can add decorations.

9. Decorate the magnificent dragon with feathers, shells, colored stones and beads, or anything you like!

A prehistoric pterodactyl

Hundreds of millions of years ago in prehistoric times, huge reptiles soared through the air. The pterodactyl was a flying reptile with enormous, but fragile, wings that were similar to the wings of today's bats.

1. Draw the main outline of the pterodactyl onto cardboard. Go over the drawing with a black felt-tip pen. Draw the eyes and teeth on a separate piece of white posterboard, as shown.

2. Cut out the pieces you have drawn. Be especially careful when you cut around the feet, since they could tear easily. Also, cut out the eyes and teeth.

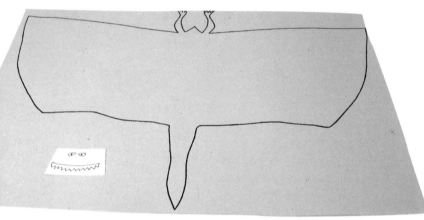

You will need:
- white posterboard
- a black felt-tip pen
- cotton ball material
- three drinking straws
- thin wooden strips
- tissue paper
- cardboard
- a pencil
- toothpicks
- tape
- scissors
- glue

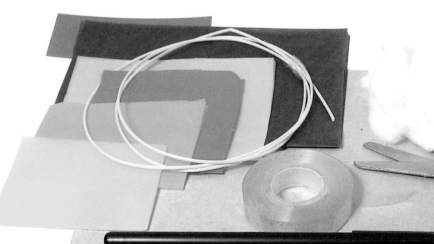

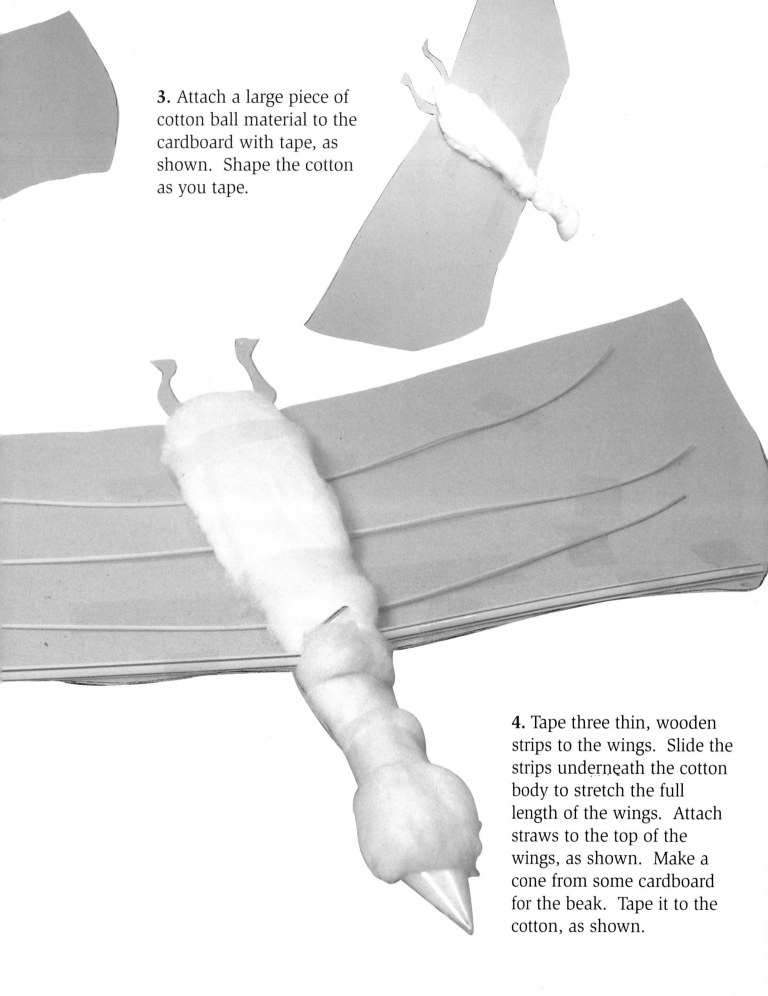

3. Attach a large piece of cotton ball material to the cardboard with tape, as shown. Shape the cotton as you tape.

4. Tape three thin, wooden strips to the wings. Slide the strips underneath the cotton body to stretch the full length of the wings. Attach straws to the top of the wings, as shown. Make a cone from some cardboard for the beak. Tape it to the cotton, as shown.

5. Put together two sets of three toothpicks, and tape these pieces into the ends of the straws as claws. Tape toothpicks onto the ends of the feet for claws.

6. Carefully glue dark brown tissue paper over the wings. Do not cover the claws.

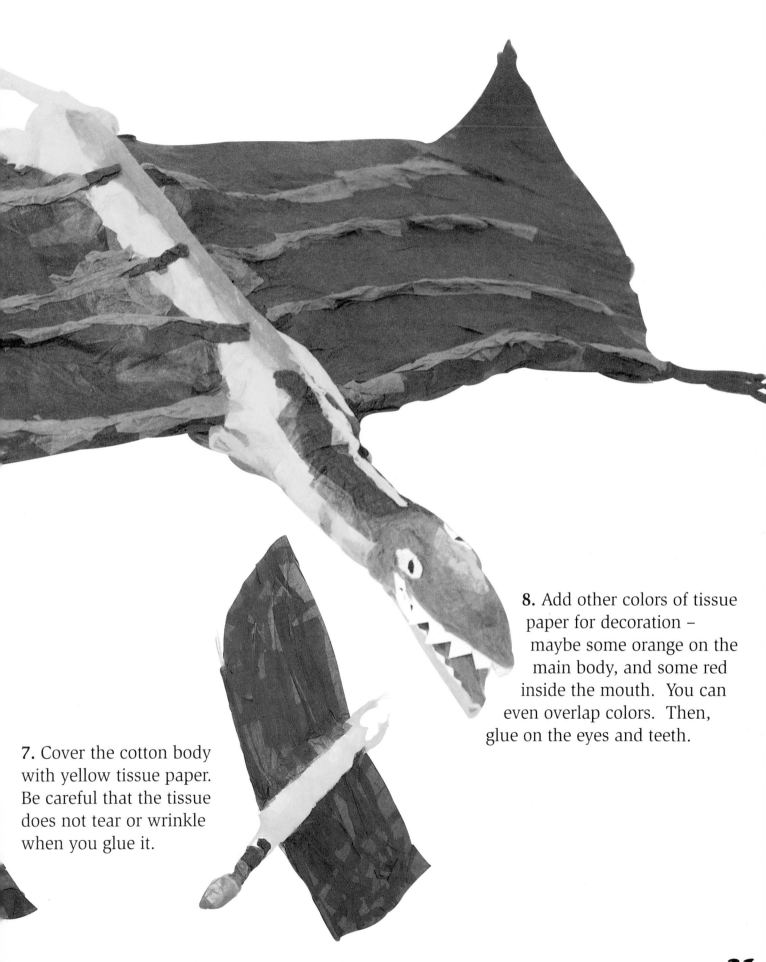

8. Add other colors of tissue paper for decoration – maybe some orange on the main body, and some red inside the mouth. You can even overlap colors. Then, glue on the eyes and teeth.

7. Cover the cotton body with yellow tissue paper. Be careful that the tissue does not tear or wrinkle when you glue it.

Glossary

architect: a person who designs and supervises the construction of buildings.

celebration: a public festival held to honor a particular event or person.

ceramic: earthenware, porcelain, or brick made from a substance, such as clay, and then baked.

fins: the thin, flat parts on the side of a water animal that help it move through the water.

Middle Ages: the period in European history from about A.D. 500 to 1450.

palette knife: a flat plastic or wooden tool used in sculpting and modeling.

papier-mâché: a modeling substance made of paper pulp. The term is French, and it means "chewed paper."

prehistoric: an event that occurred before recorded human history.

pterodactyl: an extinct flying reptile that is part of a larger group called pterosaurs. Pterosaurs had long, narrow wings made of a thin membrane of skin. Most of them lived near the sea and ate fish and other sea animals.

slip: a substance that is used to bond pieces of clay together. It is made by mixing water with clay to make a paste.

tempera paints: paints that are mixed with water.

traditions: beliefs, holidays, and customs that are passed down from generation to generation.

Books and Videos for Further Study

Dragon Mobiles. Hull (Watts)

Ghosts, Monsters and Legends. Bradley (Mad Hatter Publishing)

Learning about Dragons. Stallman (Childrens Press)

Worldwide Crafts (series). Deshpande and MacLeod-Brudenell (Gareth Stevens)

Digging Up Dinosaurs. (Reading Rainbow Video)

Dinosaur! An Amazing Look at the Prehistoric Giants. (Children's Video Library)

My Pet Monster. (Hi-Top Video)

The Reluctant Dragon. (Disney Video)

Index